J

What's [next]?

THE HARD CORE TRUTH ABOUT HOW TO GET HIRED

Printed in the United States of America

ISBN 978-0-944002-33-9

Con[ten]ts

"Success comes from doing common things *uncommonly* *well.*"

—W. Clement Stone

Job [hunt]ing

Frankly, almost all of us are amateurs at it.

If we find ourselves needing to make a career move, we may pick up a book about job search and start cramming. We might check out a couple of websites for advice on resumes or how to interview. Maybe we attend a workshop to learn techniques for finding employment.

Of course, most people just feel their way along until they land a job offer. And they make a lot of rookie mistakes.

It's not that job hunting is so complex. It's just that we don't do it on a regular basis.

Actually, searching for a new job is a game of fundamentals. We're not likely to score with some trick play, but rather by mastering the basic "blocking and tackling."

This handbook boils down the latest job-related research and gives you the know-how you need. No more "winging it." No more wasted effort on a time-consuming, trial-and-error approach.

Here's the hard core truth about job-hunting practices that work best.

Reality [check]

Successful job hunting depends on your knowing which techniques work best and why. Use this short quiz to see how well you understand the realities of the situation.

1. On average, how many hours do unemployed people spend on job search tasks each week?
   a. Less than 15
   b. 16 to 25
   c. 26 to 40
   d. More than 40

2. What is the most commonly used job search method?
   a. Replying to Internet postings
   b. Networking
   c. Cold calling
   d. Working with search firms

3. Which of the following is the least effective job search method?
   a. Replying to Internet postings
   b. Networking
   c. Cold calling
   d. Working with search firms

4. Job candidates should contact employers who are *not* hiring.
   True or False

5. What's *not* on a resume can be just as important as what's on it.
   True or False

6. The major career sites—Monster.com, Hotjobs.com, and CareerBuilder.com—are the best places to post your resume.
   True or False

7. About 30% of jobs are unadvertised.
   True or False

8. Regardless of the health of the economy, there are more than one million job vacancies in the U.S. each month.
   True or False

9. A job candidate should ask about money at an interview.
   True or False

10. The most qualified people get hired.
    True or False

11. Networking with everyone you meet is a poor use of your time.
    True or False

12. Hiring managers often decide "No" during the first five minutes of an interview.
    True or False

13. A job search is a numbers game.
    True or False

14. What's the best answer to the interview question, "Why should I hire you?"
    a. "I'm a hard worker who always gets the job done."
    b. "I deliver results. For example . . . "
    c. "I work well with others and bring out their best."

15. What should you care most about when writing your resume?
    a. Who will be reading it
    b. Choosing the right resume format
    c. Listing your qualifications

16. The most useful way to use the Internet in a job search is:
    a. Researching employers and decision makers
    b. Expanding your network
    c. Responding to job ads
    d. Both a and b

17. Even if you have been unemployed for a long time, you should make a counteroffer.
    True or False

Answers are at back of book on pages 64-65.

CHAPTER 1

Net[work]ing

Studies from a variety of sources, including the U.S. Department of Labor, rank networking as the most effective way to find employment. At least **70% of people find their jobs via their network**.

The success rates for job search methods are as follows:

Identify decision makers and network to them	70-85%
Identify decision makers, send resumes, and cold call	8-10%
Contact recruiters	6-7%
Reply to advertised postings (online and classified ads)	4-5%
Send mass mailing of resumes (no follow-up calls)	2-3%

Networking works the best for several reasons:

- There are far fewer job candidates competing for unadvertised openings. Networking is the only way for you to find these **"hidden" jobs**.

- Networking can get a job candidate on an **employer's short list** even before there is a job vacancy. Eventually, every company has a vacancy.

- Employers simply prefer to **hire referrals**. It's less expensive and less work than hiring a complete stranger.

More than **65%** *of jobs are unadvertised.*
For these jobs, it's not just what you know
*but **who** you know.*

**Use the following approach in developing
your job search connections.**

1) **Build your list of target companies.** Research and identify 25-50 companies that you are interested in working for. In your selection process, consider criteria such as each company's location, industry, growth rate, reputation, size, and culture.

Next, identify the decision makers in your target companies. Decision makers are the managers who have the power to hire you. You ultimately want to network your way to them.

The sources on the opposite page will help you compile a list of target companies and decision makers.

Online sources:

Company web sites

Press releases

Company blogs

AnnualReports.com

Forbes.com

Greatplacetowork.com

Hoovers.com

CNNMoney.com

Bizjournals.com

ThomasNet.com

Print sources:

Libraries

Chamber of Commerce lists

Local newspapers

Trade journals

Popular business books

The JobBank series

D & B Business Rankings

Standard & Poor's 500 Guide

*Guide to America's Federal Jobs:
A Complete Directory of
Federal Career Opportunities*

Even though there is more information available on large companies, don't limit your research to only them. According to *The Wall Street Journal*, "over the past decade, small businesses have created 60% to 80% of net new jobs."

2) **Brainstorm.** Make a list of everybody you know: friends, acquaintances, neighbors, relatives, church members, clergy, classmates, teachers, club members, employers, supervisors, colleagues, vendors, customers, fellow association members, consultants, lawyers, bankers, doctors, dentists, barbers, golf buddies, etc.

3) **Go public.** Contact everyone in your network. Let them know you are in the job market and the type of position you are looking for. Touch base with even the most casual acquaintances.

Gather intelligence. Since most people can't offer you a job, seek their advice.

For example, ask questions such as:

Do you have any thoughts on what the next steps should be in my job search?

Do you know so-and-so (the decision maker) or someone who does?

What companies would you look at if you were to change employers?

This is a list of employers I'm interested in. Do you know anyone at these companies?

It could take hundreds of conversations before you network your way to a decision maker. Nonetheless, your odds of landing a job through this proactive approach are much greater than finding employment through passive search methods such as responding to online job ads and mass mailing resumes.

5) **Persevere.** Expect some contacts to give you the cold shoulder. Don't let it bug you. Remind yourself that most jobs are filled through word of mouth. Continue to ask people for leads, advice, ideas, and referrals.

37% of workers polled by search firm Robert Half International said the biggest mistake people make when networking is not asking for help.

6 Be a giver, not just a taker. Show interest in your network contacts. Find out what's happening in their work and personal lives. Engage them in conversations and focus on how you can help them. Good networking is a two-way street.

7 Socialize. The last thing you want to do when you are unemployed is retreat behind closed doors. Work at keeping your social calendar full. Hang out at civic organizations, health clubs, golf courses, fundraisers, church groups, career fairs, business conferences, trade shows, etc.

8) **Become an active member of professional organizations.** Join professional associations, attend their meetings, and build relationships with other members. For just about every conceivable occupation, there's an association. *The Encyclopedia of Associations*, available at public libraries, contains information on more than 100,000 organizations. And Weddles.com offers links to over 1,000 associations.

9) **Network your way to decision makers before they need you.** Most job hunters spend all their time chasing job openings. Don't follow the crowd. Contact employers before there is an opening. Make them aware of your interest and qualifications so when they have a vacancy, you have a head start on the competition.

The majority of companies, regardless of whether they are shrinking or growing, will have job vacancies this year. People retire, move to new jobs, accept promotions, etc.

Even when the total number of jobs declines in the U.S., The Conference Board reports more than 2.5 million online advertised job vacancies each month. That number does not include the estimated additional 3 million job openings each month that are not advertised anywhere.

job openings each month that are not advertised anywhere.

10) **Internetwork.** The following are several ways to use the Internet to expand your network:

- Connect with professionals via Linkedin.com, Ryze.com, Jibberjobber.com, Brightfuse.com, and Ziggs.com.

- Become a member of online communities such as Facebook.com and Friendster.com.

- Track down former coworkers at Corporatealumni.com, Classmates.com, and Zoominfo.com.

- Participate in trade association chat rooms, industry conference discussion forums, and blogs.

- Use Technorati.com to search blogs for the names of decision makers.

11) **Cast a wide net.** Don't be snobby about who you network with. Your dry cleaner may be the brother of a corporate executive who is looking for an employee like you. *You just never know.*

Treat every individual as valuable regardless of their perceived influence. Think of it this way. Every person knows at least 100 people. Therefore, if you meet any ten new people, you immediately increase the number of your potential contacts by a minimum of 1,000 people. One of those 1,000 might be the person who helps you land a job.

> *"I'm not a snob. Ask anybody.*
> *Well, anybody that matters."*
>
> —Simon Lebon,
> of the rock band Duran Duran

CHAPTER 2

Divers [i] fying
your job search

**Networking is the way most people find their jobs, but of course
it's not the only way. So it pays to diversify your efforts.**

Using multiple search methods improves your chances for re-employment
while also making the job-hunting process less tiresome and tedious.

1) **Respond to online job ads.** It's not unusual for hundreds of applicants to apply for each online advertised job opening. The competition is fierce. Because each ad draws tremendous attention, no more than 5 out of 100 people find new jobs via online job boards.

"The majority of online job seekers spend an average of 50 hours per month searching the Internet for jobs." —Kelton Research survey

"Jobs *ranks sixth in the top ten online search terms, above* cars, games, *and* porn." —Google

"Nearly 13% of the traffic on the Internet can be traced to people visiting career job sites." —Nielsen//NetRatings

5 *out of* 100

find new jobs via online job boards

Fortunately, you can do things to improve your chances.

First, don't waste your time. Respond to job postings only when the credentials on your resume closely match the specs of the job. Employers are extremely selective because they have tons of resumes from which to choose. If you don't look like a perfect fit on paper, your chances are slim to none.

Second, if you answer a job ad and hear nothing back for two weeks, place a phone call directly to the hiring manager and reiterate your interest.

Third, focus on the online sites that fill the most jobs. Employer web sites account for the most Internet hires. Companies will first search through their own databases before they advertise openings on other sites.

Over 90% of the Global 500 companies advertise job openings on their websites.

Specialty job sites fill one-third more jobs than major career sites. There is a specialty site for practically every occupation.

Lists of niche sites are available at:
Rileyguide.com
Jobhill.com
Topjobsites.com
Job-employment-guide.com
Nicheboards.com

The big job boards, Monster.com, CareerBuilder.com, and Hotjobs.com, are among the best-known, most-used, and least-effective sites for job hunters. It's true that if you post your resume to one of these sites, thousands of employers will have potential access to it.

Unfortunately, they will also have access to millions of other resumes in the same database.

2) **Register with a recruiter.** Recruiters fill about 7% of jobs. They know which companies are hiring, and they can do the legwork to get you an interview. However, they will probably not give you the time of day unless you are a nice fit for a position they are currently attempting to fill. Nonetheless, they are worth contacting, especially the ones that specialize in your area of expertise.

Recruiters fill about 7% of jobs

Sources of free information:
Onlinerecruitersdirectory.com
Recruitersonline.com
Searchfirm.com
Headhuntersdirectory.com

3) **Consider employment agencies.** Check out agencies if you are interested in entry to mid-level positions or temporary work. Sites such as Net-temps.com and Americanstaffing.net provide links to agencies in your area.

4) **Make cold calls . . . a lot of them.** Cold calling is phoning complete strangers without a referral. You will probably have to make at least 100 calls to get through to an interested decision maker. The callers who succeed have a good 30-second sales pitch. Plus, they have the tenacity to keep dialing after repeated rejections. While the response rate on cold calls is low, it's much higher than just mailing a resume and doing nothing more.

5) **Make the postal system work for you.** Increase the odds that your cover letters and resumes bypass gatekeepers and reach decision makers. Send your mail certified. This service requires the recipient's signature at the time of delivery.

Certified mail costs a bit more, but the extra postage is worth it, especially if you are investing time to customize your message for each employer.

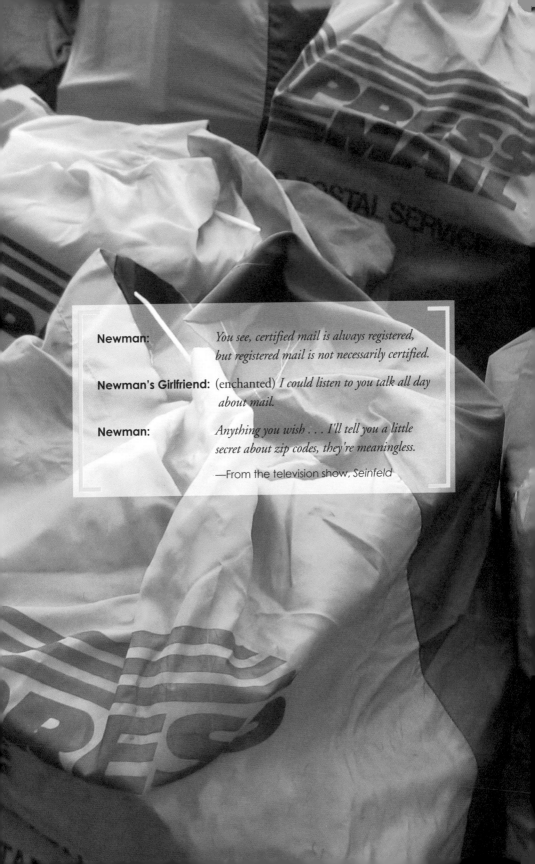

Newman:	*You see, certified mail is always registered, but registered mail is not necessarily certified.*
Newman's Girlfriend:	(enchanted) *I could listen to you talk all day about mail.*
Newman:	*Anything you wish . . . I'll tell you a little secret about zip codes, they're meaningless.*
	—From the television show, *Seinfeld*

CHAPTER 3

Cover letters

Your cover letter should be short and sweet, but provocative and powerful.

Its job is to introduce you and cue up your resume, making the employer want to read more about you.

Just as an after-dinner speaker needs someone to give a brief introduction that builds credibility, grabs the crowd's attention, and makes people want to hear what the speaker has to say, your cover letter should create interest and command attention.

1) **Always send a cover letter with your resume.** A nationwide survey by Accountemps found 60% of executives believe "a cover letter is either as important as or more critical than a resume."

2) Address for success. Don't address your letter "To Whom It May Concern." People want to see their own names. Research online or call the company to get the hiring manager's name and correct spelling.

3) Customize the letter. Employers feel good if job seekers have some connection to them. Mention the name of a personal reference to the company if you have one. Explain why the particular company interests you, and note your accomplishments that make you a perfect fit for the job.

Show that your decision to apply to the company was a well-informed one. Work a flattering fact about the company into the letter. You don't want potential employers to think that you selected them out of the Yellow Pages.

4) **Keep it to one page.** Company recruiters often have to plow through hundreds of applications. They dislike long-winded, rambling cover letters. Be succinct.

5) **Double-check.** Closely proofread your cover letter more than once before sending it, and ask someone else—a fresh pair of eyes—to do the same. The letter must be perfectly clean. One mistake can disqualify you.

6) **Avoid flowery language.** Don't write sentences you would never say out loud, such as "Enclosed is my resume for your *perusal.*" Or, "I have a *plethora* of skills." Choose your words so you come across as smart, not pretentious.

> *"What's another word for*
> *thesaurus?"*
> —Steven Wright

one page

double-check

no flowery language

CHAPTER 4

Resu me s

Your resume has two key functions, and you should design it
with both of these in mind.

First, it's a sample of your work.
The resume lets a potential employer look at something you have produced.
So here's a chance to demonstrate your work standards and ability to perform.

Second, the resume serves as your personal brochure.
It's a sales pitch about you, a promotional piece showcasing why
you're an excellent candidate for the particular job you're targeting.

Follow these guidelines in developing your resume. *buzz*

1) **Make the first cut.** Technology has changed the way resumes are reviewed. More than 80% of companies now use scanning software to select resumes based on keywords identified by hiring managers. In many cases, if your resume fails to have the right keywords, it will never be reviewed by a human being.

Increase the chances your resume will get past the gatekeeper technology. Review job ads to **discover** the common **buzzwords** and **industry jargon** for the type of job that interests you. And strategically weave these words into your resume.

buzz words

2) **Be selective in what you volunteer.** What's *not* on a resume can be just as important as what is on it. Hiring managers narrow the field of applicants by looking for reasons *not* to interview people.

Therefore, do not include:

- Explanations about why you left previous employers. That could be a touchy subject, so save it for the interview.

- Your past earnings. If your compensation falls outside the range the employer has in mind, your resume will most likely get pitched.

- Short-term jobs if they don't improve your credentials. Job hopping concerns employers.

- Graduation dates from more than 20 years ago. You don't need to reveal information that will help an employer determine your age.

- Your photo or details about your personal life such as your marital status, religion, ethnicity, date of birth, height, and weight. This information might not fit with the hiring manager's preconceived notion of the ideal candidate.

- A list of references. It's not appropriate to share references before a first interview.

Always tell the truth. But don't over-tell. Your resume has only one purpose—to get you an interview.

3) **Edit ruthlessly.** Keep your resume to no more than two pages. Place your key selling points on the top quarter of the first page and carve out any repetitive information. Recruiters will initially skim your resume for no more than 15 seconds. Don't make them work hard to see you are an outstanding job candidate.

Top three common mistakes job seekers make on their resumes

Typos or grammatical errors—34%

Including too much information—22%

Not listing achievements in former roles—17%

—Poll conducted by Accountemps of 150 U.S. senior executives from a range of departments including human resources, finance, and marketing

Sweat the small stuff. An error on your resume can brand you as careless. One misspelling or grammatical goof and you may be toast.

Follow these steps to catch mistakes:

1. Print your resume. It's easier to proofread on paper than on a computer screen.
2. Check each word several times. Don't rely on your software's spell check. Your software can't tell the difference between "ruining" and "running."
3. Check formatting. Be consistent in your use of spacing and fonts from section to section.
4. Make corrections and then let the resume sit overnight.
5. Print it the next day, proof it again, and make any further corrections.
6. When you think your resume is perfect, have someone else review it.

5) **Choose the right format.** There are two basic types of resume formats:

- The **chronological format** groups your accomplishments by your employers. Employers are listed, most recent first, along with dates of employment.

- The **functional format** groups your accomplishments by your skills. The names of employers and dates of employment are not emphasized or even cited.

> **Hiring managers favor the chronological format** *because it's sequential, straightforward, and does not camouflage job hopping and career gaps. A functional format immediately raises suspicions. There is no reason to use this type of layout if you are not switching careers and your work history is stable with no long periods of unemployment.*

6) **Sell results.** Cliché terms fall flat. "Hardworking, experienced, motivated, goal-oriented team player" reads like "yada yada yada." Hiring managers want proof. Anything without facts is just an empty boast. Be very specific in how you have delivered value. Quantify your accomplishments.

7) **Customize.** Your resume is your advertisement. The first rule of advertising: Know your target audience. Emphasize different skills and accomplishments for different employers. Tailor your resume to the needs of each company. If you try to make one resume work for all organizations, it will probably work for none.

8) **Be ethical.** Thorough employers will check your degrees plus call your references and former companies. Lies, no matter their size, can kill your chances for employment. In a CareerBuilder.com survey, 49% of hiring managers reported they caught candidates lying on their resumes.

"With all the electricity we're using to keep Meredith alive, we could power a small fan for two days. You tell me what's unethical."

—Dwight Schrute,
commenting about a coworker in the hospital.
From the television show, *The Office*

Preparation

Preparation

Preparation

The three keys
[to a successful interview]

CHAPTER 5

Inter[view]ing

The interview is the centerpiece of the selection process.
But whether it lasts only a few minutes or for several hours, your performance will be determined largely by the work you do before coming face-to-face with the employer.

There are three stages to the interview: **Preparation, face time, and follow-up.** Most job candidates blow into the actual interview session thinking that's where they need to shine the most. Well, that's true. But you win the game on the practice field— by diligently studying the hiring organization, slanting your resume and cover letter to suit the situation, and reflecting on how to frame your interview responses in order to portray yourself as an ideal candidate.

Here are the ground rules.

1) **Research like mad.** Go the extra mile when researching potential employers. Learn about each company's history, goals, strategy, competitors, product lines, and services. Gather insights on emerging industry trends, opportunities, and challenges. Interviewers are flattered and impressed by job candidates who do their homework.

Invest at least 10 hours in research for each interview. It will be time well spent.

Your research will:
- Enable you to better talk about how you can bring value to the operation
- Show how serious you are about becoming part of the organization
- Help you ask smart questions about the job
- Demonstrate your enthusiasm, intellectual curiosity, and hustle
- Give you a competitive edge because most other job candidates will do little research, if any.

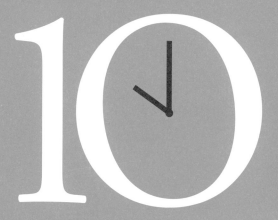

Invest at least 10 hours in research for each interview.

2) **Google yourself and your interviewers.** Run a search on your name. Make sure you know as much about your online presence as potential employers do. Also, query the names of your interviewers on Google.com, Linkedin.com, Facebook.com, and company web sites. It's easier to find common ground with hiring managers when you know something about them.

> *77% of recruiters use search engines to research candidates, and 35% disqualify candidates because of information discovered online.* —ExecuNet survey

3) **Be early.** Arriving late tells the interviewer that that you do a poor job of managing your time and planning ahead.

Get good directions to the location. Allow adequate time for traffic and parking. Plan to enter the building at least 15 minutes early. Use some of that extra time to take a restroom break and check your appearance.

4) **Look sharp.** Hiring managers often decide "No" during the first five minutes of the interview. First impressions are powerful, especially negative ones.

Show up looking your best. Regardless of whether you think it's fair or not, your appearance will influence the interviewer's hiring decision.

A CareerBuilder.com survey asked hiring managers to name the most common and damaging mistake made by interviewees. Over 50% responded "dressing inappropriately." Err on the side of formality. You will be at an uncomfortable disadvantage if your interviewer is dressed nicer than you.

5) **Take the high road.** Be honest about why you left your previous job, but don't dwell on the subject. Keep your explanation short and to the point. Share what have you learned from the experience, and then move on. Do not, under any circumstance, trash former employers. In fact, find only good things to say. Put a positive spin on your past and the people in it.

6) **Give off good vibes.** If you have any reservations about the job or organization, keep them to yourself at the interview. Negativity is the kiss of death. Be relentlessly positive about the company and show some real excitement about the opportunity. In a close contest, the candidate who appears to want the job the most will land the offer.

7) **Tell the truth.** Even a white lie or small exaggeration can come back and bite you. Comprehensive background checks have become routine.

8) **Commit your answers to memory.** Expect to hear these staple interview questions or variations of them:

- What can you tell me about yourself?
- What are your greatest strengths? And weaknesses?
- Why are you interested in working here?
- Why should we hire you?
- Why did you leave your previous positions?
- What do you want to be doing five years from now?

Draft your responses in advance. *A job interview is too important to rely on your talent for improvisation. Memorize your lines. Then, practice them out loud so they sound conversational, not canned.*

You can't over-prepare. *Your credentials mean little if you don't perform well in the interview spotlight. People who ace the interview get hired, not the people most qualified.*

9) **Prepare your stories.** Scan your memory and recall times when you excelled in the following areas: helping coworkers, solving problems, selling your ideas, saving money and time, pleasing customers, building relationships, and improving productivity. Virtually all employers want to hire people who can do these things well.

Use actual stories about your accomplishments to turn common questions into memorable answers. Interviewers more easily remember stories than vague, general statements. In each story, state the problem or opportunity, the action you took, and the results achieved. Whenever possible, describe the outcomes in dollars or percentages.

10) **Keep responses to no more than two minutes.** Don't test the attention span of the interviewer. Candidates who ramble and go off on tangents literally talk themselves out of the job. Resist the urge to cover stuff that has nothing to do with your credentials.

11) **Interview the interviewer.** If you are not inquisitive during an interview, you will be perceived as having little imagination, interest, and energy. Prepare questions about both the position and the company.

Consider these:

Why did you choose to work here?
What do you like best about the company?
What were the strengths and weaknesses of the person who previously held this job?
What is the biggest challenge the company is facing in the next five years?
What do you want your team to accomplish?
What are the two most important tasks for this position in the immediate future?

Use additional inquiries to showcase your knowledge of the business. You could start the dialog as follows:

From what I have read, your company . . .

Based on my research, your competitors . . .

I recently read in a trade journal that your industry is . . .

When it comes to impressing an interviewer, your questions can be just as important as your answers.

12) **Show appreciation.** Don't hurt your chances by failing to be courteous. Within one day of an interview, send a thank you letter or email. Express your gratitude, reconfirm your interest, and emphasize something positive you learned at the interview about the employer.

What is the most unusual thing a candidate did in a job interview this year?

- Answered cell phone and asked the interviewer to leave her own office because it was a "private" conversation.

- Told the interviewer he wouldn't be able to stay with the job long because he thought he might get an inheritance if his uncle died—and his uncle "wasn't looking too good."

- Said she could not provide a writing sample because all of her writing had been for the CIA and it was "classified."

- Flushed the toilet while talking to interviewer during phone interview.

—CareerBuilder.com annual survey of 3,000 hiring managers and HR professionals

---

13) **Conduct salary research.** Prior to an interview, build the equivalent of a *Kelley Blue Book* for your position. Gather salary data for similar jobs for someone with your education and experience in your city. The following sources can help you determine the going market rates:

Online sites:

Salary.com   Payscale.com

Bls.gov   Salaryexpert.com

Job boards and classified ads that mention salary figures for similar positions

Networking contacts who know the salaries of comparable positions in other companies

Recruiting firms that specialize in your industry or profession

Don't volunteer your salary research at an interview. There will be plenty of time to talk about compensation if you are extended an offer. Initiating discussions about money beforehand could leave the impression that you care more about yourself than making a contribution. An interview should be about what you can do for the company, not what the company can do for you.

Besides, you don't want to tip your hand. If you reveal a salary number to your interviewer, you could commit yourself to a lower figure than the employer would have otherwise offered. Or you could take yourself out of contention by asking for too much.

What do you do if an interviewer asks about your required salary? Consider one of these responses:

" My salary requirements are open. I am more interested in the challenges and opportunities of this position."

" I'd like to earn a salary equal to the value I can bring this organization."

" Salary is important but not my only consideration. I'm also interested in the whole package, including benefits and future opportunities."

You should hedge only once or twice. If the hiring manager presses you for an answer, provide one. You can answer with some confidence because of your pre-interview salary research. Make sure you provide a salary range rather than a specific number. Give yourself some maneuvering room if you get an offer.

"I earn a seven figure salary.
Unfortunately,
there's a decimal point involved."
—Bumper Sticker

CHAPTER 6

Offers ... and [Counter] offers

Sooner or later, if things go well, the conversation turns to money.
At this point you need to **be a negotiator as well as a salesperson**.

This phase of the selection process makes many candidates uncomfortable.
The main reason? They've failed to do their homework. So they don't even know
the right price tag to put on themselves.

Here's where your salary research pays off in actual dollars and cents.
If you've figured out how the compensation compares for similar positions in your
geographic area, and if you are prepared to highlight the abilities you would bring
to the job, you're in a position to negotiate effectively.

1) **Know how low you will go.** Determine the absolute worst compensation terms you would be willing to accept for the position you are seeking. Factor your salary research, financial needs, and career goals into your analysis.

2) **Be deliberate.** When extended an offer, do not decide on the spot. Request two days to evaluate the compensation package. Buy yourself some time to prepare a thoughtful response.

3) **Evaluate the deal in its entirety.** Benefits and perks are generally 15% to 20% of the value of an offer. Don't get so wrapped up in a base salary number that you fail to evaluate the rest of your compensation package. Non-base salary components of a compensation package can include:

- Commissions
- Stock options
- Bonus and profit sharing
- Pension plan
- Health, life, and dental insurance
- Vacation and sick days
- Education cost reimbursement
- Moving expense reimbursement
- Parking
- Laptop computer
- Severance pay
- Timing on eligibility for pay increases
- Flexible work schedule
- Organization memberships
- Fitness club memberships
- Training
- Wellness programs
- Employee Assistance Programs

Think beyond the start date. Picture yourself in the job. Will you work well with your boss? Is the chemistry right? Will you enjoy the work? Will it give you a sense of achievement? Will you acquire valuable skills and experience? Will the job advance your career?

Look down the road. Your starting salary compensation certainly matters, but so does your career growth and satisfaction.

In a recent About.com poll, people were asked "What gives you the most job satisfaction?"

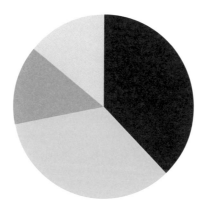

● I love what I do	38%
○ Respect from my boss	34%
◐ The amount of money that I make	14%
○ I don't get satisfaction from my job	14%

5) **Ask for more money.** In a Society for Human Resource Management survey, "80% of hiring managers said they were willing to negotiate salary and benefits. Yet, only 33% of job applicants said they were comfortable negotiating."

Even if you have been unemployed for a long time, don't be shy about making a counteroffer. However, be realistic. Your suggested salary range should not wildly exceed the numbers gathered from your research.

6) **Sweeten the pot.** Request extra perks such as additional vacation days, earlier eligibility for raises, etc. Place multiple requests on the table so you can concede a few. One of the best ways to negotiate for a fatter paycheck is by negotiating for other things as well. You don't want your base salary to be your only bargaining chip.

7) **Act like the employer "had you at hello" . . . except on the issue of compensation.** Let the hiring manager know your only reservation is the compensation package. Express enthusiasm for the job, the organization, and its people. Your positive energy strengthens your negotiating leverage. An employer is more likely to make concessions to a job candidate who is excited about the opportunity.

8) **Continue to sell.** Justify your asking price. Highlight your previous accomplishments, especially the instances when you made or saved money for previous employers. Plus, share the research that supports your position. Salary numbers from objective sources can be very persuasive.

"The efforts of job applicants to negotiate higher salary and benefits result in an average 15% increase in compensation."

—U.S. Department of Labor

If a job candidate spends one hour to successfully negotiate a 15% raise on a $40,000 base salary, the $6,000 annual increase adds up to $30,000 of earnings over the next five years. There are not many things a person can do to earn $30,000 per hour, other than negotiating compensation. Or playing in a Super Bowl.

9) **Preserve the relationship.** Approach negotiations with a cooperative, friendly attitude. Set a positive tone. Work on crafting a deal that makes the employer feel good. Never issue ultimatums or fuss about petty issues. You don't want to win concessions and antagonize your future boss in the process.

80% of corporate headhunters said the job candidate who negotiates in a constructive way is more impressive than one who accepts the first offer or negotiates in a demanding manner. —Careermag.com survey

10) **Bring the negotiations to a conclusion.** If you sense frustration from the other side, or if you've completed three rounds of back and forth negotiations, make a decision. If the deal exceeds your bottom line requirements, accept it. Otherwise, walk away. Regardless of what you decide, be respectful and appreciative.

11) **If you reach agreement, get it in writing.** Request a contract from the employer that covers the details of your employment, including your start date, salary, benefits, and job duties. Double-check to make sure any concessions you achieved are documented. Make sure everyone is on the same page.

> *"Sometimes, I think you have to march right in and demand your rights, even if you don't know what your rights are, or who the person is you're talking to. Then, on the way out, slam the door."*
>
> —Jack Handey

CHAPTER 7

Score keep ing

It is said that **"Feedback is the breakfast of champions."** You'll be a far better competitor if you set specific job-hunting goals and closely track your daily activities.

Remember, you have a new set of duties during this career transition period. Your work has changed dramatically, so you need to set performance standards for the role you're now playing.

Spend forty hours a week on your job search and record what you're doing on a daily basis.

The end result—landing a job—will take care of itself.

JOB SEARCH SCOREBOARD

DATE_____	GOAL	ACTUAL
Total hours spent on search		
Networking phone calls		
Networking emails		
Professional association meetings attended		
Thank you notes sent to networking contacts		
Hours spent networking		
Referrals from networking contacts		
Conversations with recruiters		
Hours spent researching target companies		
Decision makers identified in target companies		
Phone calls to decision makers in target companies		
Customized cover letters and resumes mailed to decision makers		
Customized resumes posted to target company web sites		
Meetings with decision makers at target companies		
Responses to advertised openings when resume closely matches job specs		
Customized cover letters and resumes mailed		
Hours spent preparing for interviews		
Face-to-face interviews		

The greater the numbers you post to this scoreboard, the more likely you are to succeed. Ultimately, your job search is a numbers game.

*" I don't worry about not hitting.
I go to the plate every night
and I take my bat with me."*

—Terry Pendleton,
Former National League MVP

ANSWERS: A JOB SEARCH QUIZ

1. On average, how many hours do unemployed people spend on job search tasks each week?
    a. Less than 15
    According to multiple surveys, on average, people out of work spend only 10 to 15 hours on search tasks each week. In fact, a major reason people fail in their job search is because they don't put enough effort into it. So instead of slacking off, sleeping late, or watching a lot of television, work full time on your search. Clock 40 hours a week.

2. What is the most commonly used job search method?
    a. Replying to Internet postings
    It's not unusual for hundreds of applicants to respond to an online job ad. According to Nielsen//NetRatings, "nearly 13% of the traffic on the Internet can be traced to people visiting career job sites."

3. Which of the following is the least effective job search method?
    a. Replying to Internet postings
    Only 5 out of 100 people find their jobs via online job boards. The success rates of many other job search methods are higher.

4. Job candidates should contact employers who are *not* hiring.
    True
    Contacting decision makers before there is a job opening can give you a head start on the competition. The majority of companies, regardless of whether they are shrinking or growing, will have job vacancies this year. Employees retire, move to new jobs, accept promotions, etc.

5. What's *not* on a resume can be just as important as what's on it.
    True
    Do not include a photo or personal details such as your marital status, religion, ethnicity, date of birth, height, weight, etc. This information might not fit with the hiring manager's preconceived notion of the ideal candidate.

6. The major career sites—Monster.com, Hotjobs.com, and CareerBuilder.com—are the best places to post your resume.
    False
    Company and specialty web sites fill more jobs than the largest career sites.

7. About 30% of jobs are unadvertised.
    False
    More than 65% of jobs are unadvertised. For these jobs, it's not just what you know but *who* you know.

8. Regardless of the health of the economy, there are more than one million job vacancies in the U.S. each month.
    True
    Even when the number of jobs declines in the U.S., the Conference Board reports more than 2.5 million online advertised job vacancies each month.

9. A job candidate should ask about money at an interview.
   False
   If you get into a discussion on compensation at an interview, you might be asked for your required salary. If you reveal that number, you could commit yourself to a lower figure than the employer would have otherwise offered. Or you could take yourself out of contention by asking for too much.

10. The most qualified people get hired.
    False
    Your credentials mean little if you don't perform well in the interview spotlight. People who ace the interview get hired, not the people most qualified.

11. Networking with everyone you meet is a poor use of your time.
    False
    Treat each contact as valuable regardless of their perceived influence. Every person knows at least 100 other people.

12. Hiring managers often decide "No" during the first five minutes of an interview.
    True
    First impressions are powerful, especially negative ones.

13. A job search is a numbers game.
    True
    The more productive search activities that you complete, the greater the chances you will find a job.

14. What's the best answer to the interview question, "Why should I hire you?"
    b. "I deliver results. For example . . . "
    Hiring managers want proof. Provide specifics on how you have delivered value in the past.

15. What should you care most about when writing your resume?
    a. Who will be reading it
    Customize your resume to the needs of each employer. You don't want potential employers to think that you selected them out of the Yellow Pages.

16. The most useful way to use the Internet in a job search is:
    d. Researching employers and expanding your network
    A survey by Kelton Research found that "the majority of online job seekers spend an average of 50 hours per month searching the Internet for jobs." Yet, only 5% of people get their jobs via online job boards. The Internet is most effective as a job search tool when used to research companies and find new contacts.

17. Even if you have been unemployed for a long time, you should make a counteroffer.
    True
    A Society for Human Resource Management survey found that "80% of hiring managers were willing to negotiate salary and benefits with job applicants." Even if you have been unemployed for a long time, don't be shy about making a counteroffer.

[About the Author]

Joe Aberger is President of PRITCHETT, LP, a management consulting and training company in eight countries that assists Global 1000 companies with downsizings, mergers, acquisitions, and restructurings. Formerly Chief Financial Officer of PRITCHETT, he is a C.P.A. with a Masters Degree in Finance. Joe lives in Dallas, Texas, with his wife, Jennifer, and their two children.